Zoe Caw

C000060592

L;fe beats
On

Poetry book on mental health

<u>*A message about the author-*</u>

Those of us fortunate enough to know Zoe have experienced a rare and beautiful soul. Zoe lost her childhood and adolescence to serious mental health difficulties, and although the world has shown Zoe little kindness, she has always fought with compassion and courage for those in need. With her powerful and personal poems Zoe offers kindness and kinship. This book is a gift to those in need of connection, from a poet with an unlimited capacity for love.

We need to change

They talk about the depression
that goes on in your head.
But they don't talk about the depression
that makes you put a smile on instead.
The depression where it appears that nothing is wrong.
Where you try your hardest to just stay strong.
We live in a society where it should stay hidden.
As if depression or feeling sad is forbidden.
Men are made to feel like they can't talk about it
because they need to be tougher.
Feeling as if they are not allowed to suffer.
More and more kids are struggling as time goes on.
Not much help around so the road for them is so long.
We need to make a change
and maybe that one-day mental health, depression.
It's okay to say.
It's okay to say do you know what today was a really bad day.
We need to make a change so people aren't alone
. Where people feel safe in their own homes.
We need to make a change so that men speak out,
that they are strong for that there is no doubt.
And when people are sad we don't just tell them to be happy.
That we don't blame them if they get a bit snappy.
We need to make a change to let people know
that they are not alone.
Tell them to be braving
and we will always remind them that no matter
what their life will always be worth saving.

Dear the person who's completing taking their own life,
I know you're hurting
I know you feel alone
I know the future holds a lot of unknowns.
I know you may feel like there is no point,
I know you may feel pressure to not disappoint.
I know you feel a burden
, I know you feel a pain.
I know you feel like these feelings you can't explain.
I know that it feels like your never going to be okay.
And it makes you wonder if you want to stay.
I know it feels like is everyone hates you
and won't care if you're gone.
But because of you they smile
whenever they hear that certain song.
The one you told them to listen to.
Because of you someone smiled and you never even knew.
You make the world a better place
and I know your questioning if that's true.
Because this is written by somebody who doesn't even know you.
Nobody wants you gone they want you to carry on.
It's a scary road to take.
But one day you will get a break from a mind
that's been so cruel to you.
Making you question everything you do.
I know you want to fly but please just try.
Reaching out is brave not weak. So help go and seek.
I know it's easier to listen to your head but Instead
listen to me I know how much you want to be free.
Life isn't easy.
Just take someones hand who will try to understand
, to help you get out of the dark if you go now it'll leave a mark.
Keeping on going is difficult to do I know right now
you haven't got a clue how to get through.
Just take it day by day even if it isn't okay because
one day the pain will fade away please choose to stay;

From a person who doesn't/didn't want to carry
on but stayed strong even when it felt wrong
or didn't feel like she belonged.

Today

5

Life isn't an easy road to take
and sometimes you may make a few mistakes
It may feel like that it is the end,
but you never know what's just around the bend.
There may seem like there is no light,
and like you have very little fight.
I'm not going to say that you have to live because of me.
I'm not going to deny
how much you just want to be free.
But what I am going to say.
Is to live life for you.
As a life full of happiness and love,
you deserve that too.
I know it seems impossible to get through
But just know That I believe in you.
We don't have tomorrow
because it can't be guaranteed.
But you do have today if only you believe
And at the end of the day that's all you need.
One step at a time and you will soon find.
That all you get told is lies from your mind.
You have to keep going, I know your scared.
But always know there's someone out there who cares
. And if it feels like you have no one.
Read this note and know your not alone.
And Your never going to have to face this scary
world on your own.
People say that pain doesn't last forever
, that your mood changes just like the weather.
One day you expect sun and you get the other
That's just because some days are a little more tougher.
Just know that you are aloud to sufferer.
So if you're reading this and are brave but are afraid too
Know there's someone else
that feels that way just like you.

The disguise…

When I smile when I laugh when it looks like I'm okay
sometimes that can mean I'm having a really bad day.
I mean we all do it, try to hide the fact that we've cried.
Hide behind a disguise And put on a show so no one else knows.
How are you? I'm fine even though my mental health is on the line.
But everyone's feelings Is more important
and validated than mine. So my answer is always I am fine.
But sometimes when I have that smile on my face.
The smile that people says lights up a room
I'm trying to get through all the doom and gloom.
But when I have that smile on my face
and I just stare into space
I just wish someone would tell me you don't have to be strong
That when people are laughing you don't have to play along
. That you already belong.
Crying or smiling either is okay because we wouldn't have you any other way.
I don't want someone to tell me it's okay
because it isn't it's far from it. Not even a bit
, I don't even want anyone to say it'll be okay in a day or so
when they don't know.
I just wish someone would look at me see-through
and say you're not on your own.
And the future yes holds a lot of unknowns
but you don't have to go through that alone.
And one day you will find your home.
I know it seems hopeless like there is no point, but let your self be voiced.
I know you don't like people to care but that is there choice.
Smile when your happy, cry when your sad the world won't think you've gone mad.
They won't think your insane for expressing your pain.
In fact they may just do the same

Sit down and breathe

You know if you woke up today
And all you do is try to be okay
Then that's fine.
Just look after your mind.
If you couldn't shower just take it hour by hour.
And see how it goes.
It's okay if you stay in bed
and watch loads of shows who's going to know.
If you don't get all you needed to do done
It's okay if you just lay out in the sun.
Please don't drive yourself insane
You can't help that you're in pain.
Just because people may not be able to see it
doesn't mean it's not there.
Don't think that no will care.
Don't push yourself to be better.
When today you are feeling under the weather.
It's okay to have a down day.
It's okay to say
I'm going to take this day for me.
I just want people just leave me be.
Today I'm taking a step back
because I've been feeling like I'm coming of the tracks.
You need days like this
. To look after you.
Don't think people are judging you for everything you do.
Go to sleep tonight and wake up tomorrow and try again.
Maybe tomorrow you'll be in less pain.
Sometimes life can feel like an uphill climb.
And it doesn't feel like you can keep going.
Sometimes all you can do is have a little faith.
And know you deserve a break.
Tomorrow is a whole new day.
And any way that is ages away.
Go watch Netflix, put on some joggers and grab a cup of tea.
Just sit down and breathe.

Survival mode

When people tell me I am strong.
I want to tell them that
, that word doesn't belong, in the definition of me.
People say you haven't come this far to only come this far.
You've used so much strength.
I mean you could go on to be a star.
With the poetry I write. But my words of the poems
are just words of my pain on a page which I'm trying to explain.
You see strength isn't what's got me here
I've been in fear.
All my life pretty much.
To be honest I've been feeling out of touch.
I escape the reality because it's too painful.
So I put on a smile do what people expect and I get told I am able.
But I am not.
I have adapted to pain which may sound insane but I have.
You see I keep going when it's hard because I'm used to it.
I'm used to the pain
I'm used to the tears I'm used to being in constant fear.
I live my life in survival mode.
Life for me hasn't really been an easy road
I mean has it been for anyone.
People just tell me I'm so young.
And so much ahead.
Sometimes I don't even want to get out of bed.
Im scared of getting older
But people tell me I've just be bolder.

There isn't another way...

When sadness is all you've known
Happiness can be far out of your comfort zone.
You've got comfortable in the uncomfortable
because without pain who are you? And what do you do?
You fear the possibility of happiness
but the sadness you are drowning in
and you think there's no way you're going to win.
You can't live you can only exist.
You can only survive and just about get by.
So what do you do?
And people say they know and understand
when how when they are not in your shoes.
I believe there is a possibility of happiness
for you even with everything you have been through
. I'm yet to experience that too.
Sometimes you just have to have faith and be brave
even when you are so afraid.
And that's easy for me to say
But there isn't another way.

Fight today don't delay...

You may say you'll fight tomorrow
But if you don't fight today there may not be a tomorrow.
You may not understand what I'm trying to say.
Because you think you'll be okay.
But each day your not fighting it's getting deeper into the darkness
Which may seem harmless to start with.
But it won't take long and as time goes on it'll be harder to fight.
But just remember there will always be light. But you have to let it in.
You may not see the light right now
but that doesn't mean you quit, that doesn't even mean that that is it.
It just means you have a few more steps little steps to others
but massive steps for you but not impossible to get through.
One day soon you will step in the sun
And you'll have no reason to run.
I know how tiring it can be and I know how much you just want to be free.
But fight for today not for tomorrow.
Because at the end of the day that's all we have is today.
Don't think tomorrow maybe this maybe that
. Your mind is talking crap
. Tomorrow isn't guaranteed, but today is indeed
, You just have to believe
. Maybe today you're fighting monsters or demons and that's okay.
You fight even when you don't want to.
Even when your in fear that's when you do it.
Maybe fear doesn't have to be bad
which I know may sound mad but maybe fear is a good thing maybe
it'll help you win.
If you fear that means you care because
you fear that maybe your going to lose the thing you care about.
Fear is powerful and scary there is no doubt
. Like we are going on a bear hunt.
We can't go under it we can't go over it we have to go through it.
We always just have to go through it.
As painful as it may seem,
one day your smile will beam.
And you will look back and all the things you have been through.
And you did that. You
. You fought for today.
And you stayed
. That's what you call a real hero.
When you stayed strong through it all.
And stood tall faced the monsters and looked them dead in the eye
. And said I am no longer going to let you make me sit in bed all day and cry
. I am going to survive.
You may knock me down
. But I'll live for today because there may not be a tomorrow.
Fight for today. Fight to stay.
Always.

Let the love in…

I was scared to care and love or to be cared for and loved.
Because I didn't feel enough.
I didn't know how anyone could love me
I wanted people to leave me be.
Because if you let people in you could potentially lose.
And that is not something that you can not choose.
But it's better to have loved than not at all.
Even if the love was so small
Love and care doesn't need to give you a scare.
People love you and you don't need to know why.
People caring may make you want to cry.
Just because you may not like
you doesn't mean that they have to hate you too.
Maybe some people have let you down
but others can turn that around.
If you let them in of course.
Which you may have to use a lot of force
Trusting people is hard to do.
You don't want to be betrayed or lied to.
Maybe you think it'll be easier on your own.
But you don't have to be alone.
Maybe someone can love and care for you
and for you to be shown.
To be shown the love and care that you should have got.
That should have already been there
It's not a reflection of you but them. Always remember that.
Let the love in, let people care about you.
Because you deserve that. You deserve that too.

Humour…

Humours very good at hiding how we feel
.Sometimes people who are really funny
makes us laugh till our belly's kill.
You think there happy and got it all together.
But really they are feeling under the weather.
They know what it's like to feel sad and they
don't want anyone else to feel that way
. So a smile they produce to try and
take other peoples pain away.
But the happy person you know there emotions they just don't show.
They don't want anyone to know.
Because there okay on there own.
At least that's what they tell themselves.
The person who laughs and makes jokes
again and again.
Just needs someone to be there now and then.
So when you see the person smiling and you ask them are you okay.
And I'm fine they say.
Tell them I see you.
I see what you do.
The person who's laughing isn't happy all the time.
You just got to be kind.
And remind yourself
everyone has a story and demons that they hide
. And sometimes when people say there okay they've lied.
Making people laugh even when you're
in pain yourself is a very special gift
never let that get missed.

The power to get through…

When you've got so much going on in your head.
It's so hard to say do you know what
I'm going to fight for another life instead.
Because you think what is the point?
With so many people you just don't want to disappoint.
I see your pain
. It hurts so much you don't know how to explain.
But it's okay. I know how it feels.
Where nothing seems to feel real.
You are lost and scared
and don't know what to do
and no one will understand because they are not in your shoes.
But do you know what?
I do.
And I know that you have the power to get through.
It's scary I'm not going to lie.
But just look up to the sky and see the sun.
And think of your life as if you've just begun.
You can start fresh you can do your best
to create the life of your dreams,
and it could be the brightest life you have ever seen.

Autism

My mum said it's raining cats and dogs out side,so
there I went to hide terrified.
But she sat down beside me and
said it means something else instead,
She calmly said it doesn't mean cats and dogs
It's an expression to say it's raining heavily
but I take things literally.
I have autism you see.
Sometimes I get overwhelmed in crowds
or places that are loud,
Autism isn't a diagnosis I'm afraid to say I am not Autism
I have autism,
And that is okay.
But it is hard sometimes.
Eye contact can be hard to maintain at times
it's not like I'm being rude or unkind
it's just well it's part of my mind.
I can struggle understanding people's emotions
and feelings and also maybe my own but like any
other condition or struggle I shouldn't have to deal with it alone.
Change of routine is hard I struggle with change
if I need to change my routine it maybe hard to rearrange,
But if I'm honest not much is different from you and me
I just have autism you see.
You just need to understand my struggles
and help me get through and I am a person just like you.
Autism is not a disease or a reason to stay away
It just means my Brain works in a different way
I have autism and that is okay.
I smile I laugh I am still a person please try
and understand me so my struggles you don't
unintentionally worsens.
I may do things in a different way
but I have Autism and that is okay…

Struggling to breathe

I was struggling to stay,
I couldn't imagine things being okay
but I just told myself just one more day…
'Well your alive so you must want to be here'
But everyday I wipe away my own tears.
I look like I'm on top form but this pain this is norm
, my norm. I just perform.
It wasn't a simple question wether to stay
or leave but no matter the oxygen in the air I was still struggling to breathe.
My mind saying your unworthy and no good
I wish there was someone who just understood.
The helper needs help from time to time.
The comedian needs someone to tell him/her a joke from time to time.
A nurse needs medication from time to time.
From time to time we need someone
to be kind because from time to time
we all have stuff going on in our minds.
We all need someone to hold our hands that is going to try there best to understand
The screams you cannot here, the pain you cannot see.
But that doesn't mean I shouldn't get believed.
Doesn't deny how much I want to be free.
So if you see someone who is suicidal
or doesn't want to be here, but still are here
They are battling, believe me they are battling hard, so their pain please don't
disregard
Don't tell them that isn't how they feel
because to them this pain, is pain to them is really real

Is it worth it?

Sometimes you may ask your self
is it worth keeping ongoing.
Even though your full well knowing.
What the future holds.
But sometimes you just have to be bold.
You may not want to fight.
You may not want there to be light.
But even if you don't want to keep going you do it anyway.
You look fear dead in the eye and say.
I'm going to be okay.
And you don't need to believe it you just need to do it.
Take it bit by bit.
What have you got to lose?
This life you can choose.
What To do who to be.
You just have to set yourself free.
I know it's hard.
And it's not as easy as accepting the past.
But just know that feelings don't last.
But you know no one is going to give up right?
They aren't going to give up without a fight.
You will always be worth saving
in someone's eyes look
no ones going to sit and let you die.
But I know your head will tell you they will
And I'm not denying that's how you feel.
I know these thoughts and feelings feel real.
But thoughts cant kill you.
It may feel that way but please just choose To stay
not for me but for you
. Because you have so much left to do.

Through my teenage years.
I've had a lot of fears and I wiped away my tears.
I got told to be strong even though it felt wrong
with my head telling me different things it will always try to win.
The voices are loud sometimes I feel up in the clouds
. And it feels like I can no longer go on.
But I have. I always have.
I've come all this way.
And I'm going to choose to stay.
No matter how loud the voices are I've come this far
. And I'm not given up yet.
And if people want to say
I'm not strong enough say do you want a bet?
I've been in a dark place
and have had ways of coping just in case.
But now I can let go because now
I've learnt it's okay if the voices
want to shout I'm going to live anyway.
That I'm going to believe
I'm not all these things.
That I'm going to win.
And no one can take that away from me.
I'm going to learn to be free
I'm not saying it's going to be easy.
In fact, it's going to be really hard.
But I'm strong enough to get through
Because it's something I have to do.
To make the monsters go away you have to stand up
and fight and one day you'll see the light.
And not just for one day and that's it
You just have to take it bit by bit.
All we have is today
and yes the monsters may not always go away.
And it's okay to be afraid.
But you have to choose to
live because so many people love you.
Don't do the things your head tells you to.
Your head is telling you lies so
Stand up look the monster dead in the eye
And choose to fight.
Always.
It's okay to be afraid you just got to be brave.
One day things will be okay.
Be there to see it don't quit.

Jigsaw puzzle

You know a jigsaw puzzle
And all the pieces are in a muddle.
And all the pieces are not the same.
And you put them all together
and a beautiful picture it became.
The blue pieces are with the red pieces and not apart.
Because why should they be separated because
of the colour when they're together they can create art?
Each piece of the puzzle has a different role to play.
When they come together a beautiful display is made.
So if the shade is different to the other then that is okay.
Just try to listen to what I have to say
We are like a jigsaw puzzle
All in a bit of a muddle
But it's only when we come together.
That we can create the beautiful picture
that can stay that way forever.
But the thing we need to accept
is not all pieces will be like the other
, some maybe bigger then another,
or some maybe a different colour.
But that doesn't mean they don't belong
and when you put the pieces together
and it's a perfect fit you can say that they are wrong.
That's why It is important to work
as a team as you can create the most beautiful Picture ever seen.
If all the pieces were the same
it would be boring so go exploring.
Look for different and your puzzle
is going to look magnificent.

Do you know what's so hard to do
Letting go of what you're used to.
The person your trauma has made you become.
And each day that goes by your head has won
Because you just feel done.
You don't know who you would
be without the pain.
So you choose to stay.
Even though it drives you insane.
You want to be free but who will You be?
You just want to escape reality.
Letting go of illness when it's all you've known
. It's hard to let that go.
But I'll tell you who you will become.
You will become a beautiful person
Even if you have scars on your arms
It makes you even more beautiful
It shows the world you survived.
And now you're going to thrive.
And I don't think there's anything
more beautiful then that.
So if someone judges you for
those scars on your arms
You look them in the eye
and say these are just prove
I survived the storm
. You let go of what you thought was the norm.
So maybe letting go will be the best thing
you ever did. And maybe now
you can let that little kid live.

Paper cuts

At 20 to 10 I sat on the floor in a hospital bay.
Packing my things to go to where I'm going to stay.
I was sorting through my paper and all of my things.
Scared and unsure to what the future will bring.
As I was doing this my hand starting to sting.
Due to a paper cut which you could barely see
But there more painful than they may seem to be.
A cut so small, but it really does hurt you.
But people tell you just carry on the do
the things you're meant to do.
It maybe so unnoticeable to other people.
But to you. Although it doesn't look deep.
It's the cut that can kind of make you weep.
And in life we all get paper cuts
. Now I'm not talking literal but sometimes
we have things going on in our life's that are so small.
A paper cut is pain known by all.
Now if we compared that to reality and to just be kind
. And that everyone has things going on in there life's.
We all have paper cuts
. So small but hurts deep to the core
. And we don't know why on earth a cut that small would hurt for
. But it does.
It truly does.
So if you don't think your pain is valid
or you judge someone because
what there going through and it seems so small to you.
Then remember the paper cut.
And just keep your mouth shut.
Don't judge a book by it's cover.
You never know what things about them you will discover.
They may need to time recover.
A paper cut is so small yet it is the most painful cut of them all.

Happiness can be painful. Yes,
that's right happiness can be painful.
But surely if I ever experience happiness
I should just be grateful.
What even is happiness?
How does it feel?
Surely being happy is ideal.
But sometimes it can actually cause pain.
Which I know sounds insane.
You don't want to be sad,
you are just comfortable there.
Comfortable with unhappiness
, and sadness and anything other
then that gives you a bit of a scare.
You don't know why that is.
I guess you've been sad for so long
ever since you were a kid.
You kind of get used to it I guess,
and all the things you went through
and dealt with you have kind of repressed.
If you ever start to feel slightly happy you breakdown,
you self destruct in negative ways
because you just genuinely don't know how to be okay.
So the sadness is where you stay.
It's what you know.
So instead of letting go.
You hold on.
Because happiness feels wrong
Too afraid to be anything other then where you are.
Which sounds bizarre.
But it makes sense to you.
It's what your used to.
Happiness can be painful.

Depression

I've been hiding behind a disguise.
The pain is deep in my eyes.
A smile is what they see.
But lately I've been struggling to breathe.
Depression isn't always rain and clouds.
It's also feeling alone in crowds.
It's saying 'you're fine' even when your not.
And this is something that you do a lot.
There becomes a point where you just get too tired.
That you just lay there in the silence.
Living on auto pilot.
Too tired to cry so you watch the world go by.
With every are you okay?
You say you are fine, which is just a lie.
There becomes a point where your just too numb.
That you don't even know the person you have become.
A little girl who once saw the beauty in everything.
Now thinks growing up is a scary thing.
Thoughts that make it hard to get out of bed,
You don't wash, You just sleep in the day instead.
You push away the ones you love the most.
Put your phone on do not disturb mode.
Music really loudly and start writing on your notes.
I just no longer want to be alone.
I want to go home.

What happened to the days.

Getting out of bed started to become a struggle
and all my thoughts are in a bit of a muddle
what happened to the days jumping in muddy puddles
and sitting on grandad's knee
while he gave me cuddles.
What happened to the days
where the most painful thing was a graze.
From playing in the playground
or playing hide and seek
and your the first one to be found.
What happened to the days
Where the most embarrassing thing to
happen to you was accidentally calling your teacher mum.
And singing hymns in primary school
was the loudest you have ever sung.
What happened to the days
Where Freddos were 10p
There 99p now I believe.
What happened to the days.
Where you'd pour glue on your hand and
Pull it off when dry.
Or sitting in car playing eye spy.
What happened to the days.
Oh how things have changed.

The power of a smile.

A man who committed suicide by jumping
off the golden gate bridge
left a note that read, '
I'm going to walk to the bridge,
if one person smiles to me on the way I will not jump.'
A lot of people say if someone is suicidal
then there's not much a person can do.
But you could just smile at someone on the street.
And save there life's and you never even knew.
A distraction from there thoughts,
and maybe a smile on there face.
And then maybe just maybe they will realise
They were never meant to go in the first place.
Your smile may go a long way,
yes it won't fix everything or make everything okay.
But it may just make there day.
A random act of kindness
may be there guidance on how to stay on this earth
when there day is so grey.
So grey they thought they had enough and wanted
to fly up above.
Not realising how much they were loved.
In a world where you can be anything be kind.
If we all did that what a beautiful world could be designed.
With kindness and empathy combined.
So next time you say there's not much you can do,
remember this poem and remember a
thing so simple like a smile can help someone get through.
Not all hero's wear capes.
You may just be someone else's escape.

Dear parents and society

When are parents or society going to realise that
mental health or depression it is not a choice.
When are they are going to let their kids teenagers be voiced.
Why should there pain have to be shown
, and why should they be made to feel alone.
I mean come on parents your meant to show kids
the way but instead you just tell them that they are okay.
But let me tell you something they are not.
They come tell you, I'm really not okay.
But you tell them it's just a bad day.
You may think there attention
seeking but there hand they are reaching.
They feel unloved, they just want to be hugged.
Not to tell them it's okay because for them it isn't.
There mind is like living in a prison.
And they just wish there parents will listen.
So parents if your seeing this please don't dismiss,
help them see the light and give them reasons to stay and fight
. You don't have to fix them
you just have to be there and the first way of being there
is by being aware
Hold there hand the whole way through and always say to them
. 'I believe in you.
I know it's a battle day in day out and your scared there is no doubt
but I'm here all the way.
And I am here to stay. '
Sometimes parents struggle to accept that there child has
a mental disorder because they can't understand
because they adored him or her.
So don't ignore your child's mental health because
of pride and don't ignore the fact that your child
has sat in bed all day and cried
. Don't dismiss your daughter or sons
mental health because they may put on a
smile when deep down they've been struggling for awhile.
If your a parent reading this then what I suggest
is to do your best.
When you ask your child how are you?
And they say I'm fine sit down with them and be kind.
If your child says there struggling or having a bad day then
listen to every word that they say.
And you never know your understanding
may just go a long long way.

Dark tunnel

If your in that dark tunnel and you can't see the light.
That means that you shouldn't give up the fight
I know it may seem pointless and there is no way out
. And it's painful there is no doubt.
Everyday is the same and everyday is just grey.
And you start to question if you should stay.
To leave a world that's been so cruel to you.
Leaving you not knowing what to do.
As a kid we are scared of the monsters under the bed
but as we grow older the monsters can be in our heads
The way to defeat them is to face
them head on and to always remember to just be strong.
It's hard to be brave when you are so afraid.
But know that soon the monster will fade away
it's a hard battle to overcome
But one day soon you will have won.
You dealt with the monsters under
your bed so you will fight the monsters in your head.

Definition of you

It's difficult to accept the right definition of the person you are.
who you are in your head.
And who you are to the world.
As people tell you a different definition
of the you to what you are told.
Your head tells you one thing and people say the other.
It's hard to distinguish between one another.
I got told quite frankly the world needed me.
But this was something I didn't quite believe.
As i view my self as something different
then to what other people see.
With people saying they love me and/or care.
Not having much of that as a kid
and getting that now gives me a bit of a scare.
I don't like the person I've become I just feel numb.
But everyone tells me you have so much positive things to come.
They tell me
'You care and love everyone else.'
Now it's about time you start to look after yourself'
'You have a purpose to be here,
even when your head tells you that you want to disappear.'
You feel as if everyone hates you,
your not sure what to do.
But for some reason everyone keeps pushing
and hoping for you to get through.
It's hard to accept the right definition of the person you are.
You look down at your body and all of your scars.
The lines on your body,
salty tears flooding your eyes
. All the things going in on your mind.
Is not how you will be defined.

Make your life spectacular(Robin Williams tribute)

Robin Williams once said you've just got to be crazy,
it's too late to be sane.
Too late.
You've got to go full-tilt bozo. '
cause your only given a little spark of
madness don't ever lose that
cause it keeps you alive.'
Robin Williams was known
for being a massive comedian
, with appearing in well-known movies
such as Mrs Doubt fire,
Aladdin, Peter Pan.
He was the kind of man who would no doubt put a smile
on someone's face.
They struggled to put one on his own
but that was never really known.
Because Happiness was all he ever showed.
Looking through quotes he once said.
It kind of shows us the awareness
he was trying to spread.
Stuff like you don't know what people are going through,
So being kind is what you should do.
Or the saddest people try their hardest
to make people happy
as they know what it's like to be sad
and they don't want anyone else to
feel that way.
Sad people will always put a smile on their faces even if they aren't okay.
A happy person they portray.
As robin once said '
comedy can be a cathartic way to deal with trauma.
That's why
Robin Williams himself was such a performer.
In the words of Robin Williams,
None of us has very long on this earth,
So make your life spectacular.

Contradictory

I push people away even if I want them to stay.
I want to be alone but I don't want to be lonely
, I hold everyone I love closely.
I pretend I don't care
about someone or something even when I do.
It's easier to pretend
not to care then no one can disappoint you.
I may come across
as this hard person but believe me I am not.
It's a defence mechanism,
along with sarcasm humour
and keeping people at arm's length,
this is something I do a lot.
To break through the barrier to let my guard down.
Instead of just being the class clown.
This isn't how I choose to be,
it's just because I
don't believe there's anyone that can love me.
But I don't give them the change to.
I push them away
and always just tell them that I am okay.
To scared to make connections
because I'm too scared of goodbyes
so keeping people at a distance feels wise.
Someone said to me the things you fear can happen
anyway so what the point in just waiting for that day.
Sometimes I just don't know why
even when I push people away
Some of them choose to stay.

The climb.

When climbing a mountain that's difficult to climb.
We want to give up but on the hard days we have to
push harder and that's what we learn in time.
It isn't something we want to do but something we have to.
To keep going and going
. With our hard work not showing.
We've climbed and climbed.
But we look up to see how far we have yet to go
and what's at the top no one knows. But we don't look below.
The thing is we always look up to see
how much we have left to do.
But we don't look down to see how much we've already got through.
Feeling as if your not
getting anywhere.
Your tired. You think well stop climbing no one will care.
People may drag you down doesn't mean you
can't turn things around.
What if you do actually climb and get to the top.
And all your hard work does pay off.
What if your on that top of the mountain.
With the wind blowing in your hair.
And someone may judge you but you don't care.
You pushed through the pain, and maybe just
maybe it will encourage others to do the same.
I think the most beautiful thing is watching
someone who's been in the dark for so long who's
light has finally come on.
Who fought through there fears.
Pushed through the tears.
And continued to climb.
While not even knowing if it'll be worth it.
But just taking it bit by bit.
Climbed despite what was going on in there mind.
That's a beautiful thing. Seeing someone who
was battling hard who felt too broken.
But then they win. That's such a beautiful thing.

Anger

I always think people are angry at me that I
do everything wrong I believe.
I got told anger can come out as fear
Or because they care and it gives
them all a bit of a scare.
They don't want you to go and they're scared
they can't get you to stay they don't
want you to just fade away.
But I just tell them that I am okay.
It's easier to think that no one cares about you.
This is something that maybe your used too
That people are angry is
one of your heads lies when people
tell you there not your just surprised.
Maybe your not this person your head
makes you out to be maybe there is
something in this world you can achieve.
You just got to believe.
Now that is is not easy in fact it's the
hardest thing but truth is you can't let your head win.
And so what if there angry
you haven't done anything wrong.
You are a human being.
And you belong.

Change

Change can be a scary thing
A way to think of it maybe is to think of it a
But like spring.
If we didn't have summer or
autumn and winter too
What time of year is it we wouldn't have a clue.
Without spring the flowers
wouldn't grow and kids in
winter wouldn't be able to play in the snow.
We know that rain doesn't last forever it's a bit like pain.
Pain changes just like the weather.
Change can be scary
but it doesn't have to be a bad thing.
We never know what change can bring.
We don't live once.
We live every day.
Change is scary
but it's something in life that will never go away.
The leaves fall in autumn
so new ones
can eventually grow in time.
So maybe change isn't such a crime.
Maybe good can come out of change
It may feel strange.
The rain always stops
So farmers can grow their crops.
The sun will always shine again.
Just hang on till then.

Life's not always sunshine and rainbows

When I'm in pain I need to remind myself
What happens after it rains.
When everything feels torn
Remember after a storm a rainbow is formed.
With lots of different colours
Like yellow and blue.
I sit on the grass and look at it as the
Sun shines through.
I love all colours from purples to green.
I think colours put all together
can create the most beautiful thing ever seen.
Rainbows colours and the sun all help
Me when I have things to overcome.
I love dark colours and light and all things bright.
Colours makes it easier when you have battles to fight.
After rain there's a rainbow and the
sun means the battle you have won.

Remember the flowers…

Flowers bloom around spring and in may.
When I see the beauty of them.
It makes me feel like things will be okay.
Butterfly's fly all around them and so do all the bees
I sit there as I admire all the trees.
The sun is shining brightly.
Kites fly high above me.
Poppy's roses and Dandelions
All of these make me remind.
That even in the dark
There can be beauty found
in such places as the park.
How something so pretty can come from just a tiny seed.
It's so small so
much care is what it needs.
It may take times for the flowers to grow.
But we never know the progress the flower
is making in the soil below.
So if you can't visibly see progress
Or positive growth in you.
Remember the flowers.
And the flower is like you too.
The progress is invisible and underneath
the soil the most but that doesn't mean
we forget it's beauty and it's growth.

You don't owe anyone anything

You don't owe anyone anything.
Your on this earth just like them.
You shouldn't feel like
you have to play pretend.
I know you may feel so many feelings
That maybe the world
or society can't comprehend.
It's not your job or responsibility to fix everyone else.
It's not a selfish
act to focus on yourself.
Just because a lot of things may have gone on in the past.
Doesn't mean you don't have the chance to laugh.
You got to understand that not
everything that happens is down to you.
Sometimes it's because the people in
your life didn't do the job they were meant to do.
You've got to give yourself a break.
And know that it's
okay in life to make mistakes.
It's not the end of the world.
Maybe life isn't like what you were told.
Maybe it's not as straightforward as you thought it would be.
Maybe self acceptance is the key.
And maybe in time you can live a life
you may or not believed could be achieved.

'The helper'

If I see someone struggling I choose to stay.
And I never walk away.
I've always done that
Because I don't want anyone to be in pain.
Even if I am myself.
Being there for people is never a strain.
Although it may seem like I give good advice.
That's because there's been quite
a lot of difficult stuff going on in my own life.
I put my focus and emergent
on everyone else and I forget about myself.
I've had to deal with most things on my own.
But You don't think there's anybody
in this world that should have to go through things alone.
Everyone needs someone.
Quite a lot of the time I say that I don't.
But some people can't do this
on their own. Some need help to see the light
And need help to find reasons to fight.
So You hold their hand and guide them through
Even if no one did that's for you.
You want to be a hero and save everyone you come across
Life has given me so much loss.
So if someone is struggling i
will always Reach out my hand
and Your struggles or battles will I understand.

'Mummy, what's on your arms?'

My daughter asked me '
mummy what's on your Arms'
The marks on my body
were marks from month and years of self harm.
When she first asked me this i
didn't really have to words to say to explain
to my child those marks were from all my past pain.
For a moment I kind of felt ashamed.
But why should I be?
When these marks were from a time I
so desperately just wanted to be free.
I said to her these marks were
from a time I was battling
and at war with my mind and to my
body at times I wasn't that kind.
These marks all have a story
and a reason behind. But they
just show the battles I won
And your living proof
that those wars I've overcome.
Theses scars aren't something to cover.
Everyone's going through
things you will later on discover
You got to
know if you ever face battles
you won't be alone.
To get through know there's
always someone to listen to you.
A scar that emerges from either physical
or emotional is
just proof you can survive even in the most darkest times.
If you see someone with
these marks you just got to be kind.

Hold on

Hold on even when you don't know why.
Hold on even if holding on makes you want to cry.
Hold on just for a little longer.
Hold on because In time you will start to feel a little bit stronger.
Hold on even when you want to disappear.
Hold on when things are difficult, to
ones that are near.
Hold on even when things seem too difficult to bare.
Hold on because people do actually care.
Hold on because you have so much left to do
hold on because someone smiled because of you.
Hold on because this pain will pass
Hold one because the hurt your
experiencing now will pass
Hold on because one day you can give
hope to others who are now in your shoes.
Hold on because you have so much potential.
And you don't even have a clue.
Hold one because all I have said is true.
Because I'm trying to do the same too.
Hold on because a life full of happiness
and peace you deserve that you really do
Sometimes you think people
are judging or looking at you.
When actually this is just something
that they are thinking and believing to.
You think people are criticising everything you do.
I don't mean to be harsh or mean
But I don't think people actually care
Weather you believe you picked the wrong outfit to wear.
No one will stop and stare.
If you didn't sleep the
night before.
No one will wonder why on earth you have bags
under your eyes for.
Because truth is everyone has insecurities and things going on.
Everyone goes through the stage of not feeling like they belong.
The world is moving constantly with every
breathe you take no one is going
to be counting all of your mistakes.
When you have a thought that seems out of the the blue.
Then maybe that thought isn't actually true.
When your out walking on the streets
there loads of people you will meet.
People don't really have that much
time on there hands to judge everything you do
Remember what I said at the start of poem
this is something they are thinking too.

Dancing in the rain

I layed out in the rain,
hoping the chemicals of the rainwater would wash away my pain.
One could only dream as my salty
tears started to stream.
I had a little cry and
soon I wiped my eyes as I remembered the quote that said.
'It's all about learning to dance in the rain'
Which when I first heard it thought it sounded insane.
But I got up whist it was raining with my
music playing loudly and I was dancing proudly.
I kind of felt a sense of being free
What I need to do is to discover me.
Who do I want to be?
Life is fleeting and so can be whatever you are beating.
We just need to let go
, be open to the unknowns
and if we love someone we need to let them know
. Why wait or delay positivity and peace and the sense of freedom.
And say you'll start another
day when today you can try and get out of the grey.
Dance like no ones is watching.
Sing like no ones listening
. Just live your life because
it's only you that'll be missing.
So whenever your next in pain.
Go dance scream whatever you have
to do because it's about learning to dance in the rain.
We only live once that's all we've got.
We need to live life to the fullest
because maybe it can offer us a lot.

The beauty in life

We always focus on the bad in life and not much
of the good so many things in life that aren't understood.
It's always nice to have a bit of a moan,
But a super hero with a hearing aid called 'blue ear'
he was created by marvel comic to encourage a little boy to wear his own.
There's a lot to be seen when you look up in the sky,
sunshine, start nights and cloud and birds flying hog.
Live because the element we are comprised
of were from formed in interiors of collapsing star dust.
Lying on the grass staring at the stars is a must.
Cows have best friends, sea otters
hold hands when they sleep to keep them from
drifting apart or loosing each other when going round
the bend. Squirrels plant thousand of trees each year simply
but forgetting where they put there acorns.
The voices of Mickey and Minnie Mouse
actually fell in love and got married.
Live because when it's pouring down
with rain you can go dance out in it while
everyone thinks your insane.
Live because each year
people sing you a song for being alive.
Live because you always are given another chance to thrive.
Rise again you may not be the
same as when you were like 16
but your always given another
chance over and over to live.
Do you know what some days it's okay to have days acting
like a little kid.
Getting excited over the small things and playing with your little pup
Live because success happens after the
churning desire to give up.
Live because happiness and living your life is
showing all the people that hurt you, that you will win.
Live because your not the only person to feel the way you
do some point someone else felt that to they know how
you feel so someone will always understand you.
Live because you have been inspired by
others but other are inspired by you, you help people get through.
Live because blind people smile even
though they have never even seen
someone smile so remember
this when it feels impossible to ever have one because
you haven't been able to smile for awhile.
The worlds needs your truth and people are waiting for you to speak.
Life can be bleak.
But we only got one shot, so rise again count to 10 and breathe.
Go out there because there's nothing in your life you can't achieve.

What if?

We always say what if?
What if it doesn't go right?
What if there actually is no light?
What if my head has won?
What if these battles I can't overcome?
Why are the what ifs we tell ourselves are always bad,
why do we drive ourselves mad?
We tell ourselves this story about how things will be but in reality
all we can do is wait and see.
What if things do end up being okay?
What if the days do end up less grey?
What if your situation that causes you pain is to suddenly
change which may sound strange.
But it can happen
What if life turns out so much more beautiful
then you ever imagined.
The difficult decision we will probably have to
ever make is do we keep going even though
we are emotionally drained and our mind is strained.
Or do we give up and say we have had enough.
The what ifs we tell ourselves maybe that's a way of protection,
from rejection or maybe a form of self destruction
because some of us we don't think we deserve
good things so the bad we believe leading our heads to win.
As humans for some reason we always focus on the
negatives then the positives I don't know why we put our selves down no matter
how hard things get
Maybe we need to concentrate more
on the good now and then instead of putting
of ourselves down again and again.

Just keep swimming

'Just keep swimming' Dory once said
But in the sea was loads of deep waves ahead.
Loads of thing's in the way making it
difficult to get through.
But dory's right just keep swimming is something you must do…
Although dory had to get through many thing's on her own.
When she looked at Nemo she was finally home.
To her, she lost her home and it was
Something she couldn't find but home was more
of a feeling rather then a building
and this is something dory learnt it time.
Giving up dory could of done, but that day never come.
Everyday she just kept swimming,
even at times she didn't feel
as if she was winning
. Everyone never thought it was possible
to find her way back home because of her memory.
But she just kept swimming constantly.
Dory taught kids anything's possible if you believe.
To everyone's disbelief
Finding home dory achieved.
The sea wasn't always clear and most
of time she was in fear
But 'just keep swimming'
she said to do and this is something you should do to.

Time

Time is the most precious things we have got.
Time can mean a lot.
Sometimes if things happened a minute
later it wouldn't be the same.
Or maybe it saved us from pain.
Time is precious.
We think we live for infinity but we really we don't.
Life is shorter then we once thought.
It's not as straight forward to what we were once taught.
Life hurts. I'm got going to lie.
But that doesn't mean we just
give up and don't bother to try.
Life may sometimes makes us cry.
But we can also laugh. But sometimes
we have to forget the past.
Now I'm not saying to forgive and forget.
But pain can be left behind but it's something we have to let.
If time is all we got, and time we haven't got a lot.
We got to spend it on things we want to.
Spend time with those that love you.
Spend time creating happiness for you.
Because we all have different times
in this live, we all have things to get through.
But live each day as if it's your last.
And laugh. Life can hurt.
We can question why
we continue but it's just something we have to do.
And what you do with the time.
Well that's up to you to choose.
Time, time is precious never take that for granted.
It's your life no ones else's.
Please try look after yourself. Please try and be happy.

If your crying in the night

If your crying in the night and you can't see any light.
That doesn't mean you should give up the fight.
What you need to do is just try everything you can do to breathe and get through.
I believe in you.
Tomorrow you may feel differently
all I'm saying is try to listen to me.
One day things will be a distant memory.
So grab a tissue and wipe your eyes put some Netflix
on to make the time go by.
I know there's a massive part of you that wants to fly.
But that isn't the way out and your loved
and cared for and for that there is no doubt.
I'm not asking you to live for
me and I'm not putting any pressure on you to believe.
But I am asking you to try and live for you because
you have so much shit left to do.
And so many people believe in you even if you do not.
Believe me no matter what your head says you your loved and valued a lot.
So if your crying at night and you can't see
the light that doesn't mean you give up the fight.
Think of it a bit like a kite.
When the storm isn't that great the kite is hard
to navigate. But once the sunshine's
through controlling the kite is easier to do.
When it's the storm you have to hang on tight
and wait for the light it comes at some point we don't know when and how.
But eventually it'll always be there and this is something you know now.

All we have is today

If you love someone you tell them.
If you care about them you tell them
Even when you think you have
so many days left to say that to them.
You tell them now and never wait.
We think we have countless days.
But tomorrow is never promised.
All we have is today.
So just live life and be happy as much as
You can be. Life is never easy for anyone.
And unfortunately things
just happen that makes no sense for anyone.
So hug your loved ones tell them you love them.
And live everyday as if it's your last.
Life's to short to cry over a bowl of pasta.
Or to stay in bed because we don't see a point.
There's always a point.
It's your life.
And that can be a precious thing.
It can just take awhile for that to be found.

'Letting go is hard but being free is beautiful'
Holding on to what you've known for so
long can feel more comforting than getting rid of
coping mechanisms you get safety from.
To live in reality in a world you don't think you
belong in, freedom and happiness is what you've been longing.
But not too happy,
to fast, you believe happiness
for you will not last.
Due to everything that went on in the past.
Sometimes it's easier
to deal with what you know.
Then to let all the pain
and hurt and unhealthy mechanisms go.
Because what you
know now is what you've been taught
Through every single battle
that you have fought.
It's not that you don't want to get better,
you just don't know how and sometimes.
Happiness can be hard to allow.
Sometimes you break down and use self
destructive ways because you
genuinely just don't know how to be okay.
Freedom seems a long long way away.
Maybe letting go isn't bad thing
, why on earth let a thing that's so fucking evil like mental illness win.
What have you got to lose if letting go
and freedom is what you choose, you've got nothing to prove.
Better to live a life in pain then take the risk hey?
'Letting go is hard but being free is beautiful'
It isn't an easy thing to do but
this whole life thing isn't for anyone else but you.

Forgive

One of the hardest things to do is to forgive
someone who hasn't even apologised.
By doing this is may seem like your
letting them win
. But believe me you get the biggest prize.
The prize is your deciding to finally let go.
Of something that's been
hurting you for so long it will to begin with feel wrong.
Think of it as a glass with water in it.
Nothing changes if your just holding it for minute
. If you hold it for a day it will begin to hurt and strain.
Or for a long time it will eventually cause you loads of pain.
But nothing changes in the glass.
No more water has been added.
It will continue to hurt for as long as the cup lasts.
Because it's the longer you hold the cup that
causes the pain and it's not about
what the cup does or does not contain.
It's up to you how long you will hold the cup for.
And if you let it hurt you forevermore.
Forgiving someone even if they haven't
even apologised isn't for them its for you.
It's so you won't have to be held down
by them and you can actually
live life you want to.
You may think your letting them get away with
things but in the end you will win.
It may not feel that way to begin with
but now you can start to live and do anything
you wanted ever since you were a little kid.

Paper dolls

When someone hasn't really been loved
properly before they start to question will that happen forevermore.
They test people to see if they will stay.
Them giving up they're waiting for that day.
They get taken away from their home.
Making them feel isolated and alone.
Past around from pillar to post there just kids
who family's send away because they seem so 'difficult' to cope.
But really they just need to be loved the most.
They just discard them like a paper doll.
Making the kid feel so low.
They appear difficult to test how strong you are.
And sometimes to the family's
they push to far.
But love like this is meant to be unconditional.
You have to expect it all.
Even if you show them love and care they may still
kick and scream. But eventually when
they look up and see your still there, there smile will bleam
Now they've finally seen that
Not everyone will discard them like a paper
doll and soon they will be able to let the guard down.
The act was done really well and one
day they will have met someone who could tell
The person they are trying to be
The hard emotionless difficult person not everyone will believe.
Once a paper doll but a scared hurt needing
to be loved girl is what they will see.
They won't always be a paper doll and
one day they will be able to breathe.

It's what you know now

When mental health struggles
have been with you for such a long time.
And it's all you've known.
It can be hard to let it all go.
It makes no Sense sometimes living
In past tense.
But it's almost becomes a part of you.
Like how do you do this whole
life thing you haven't got a clue?
To stay into the comfortable
even when it can cause you pain.
A thing that's so difficult to explain.
When you've struggled
with it for so long it can almost feel like it just you
But your struggles are because of
things that shouldn't of happened
to you and your coping mechanisms
are things that helped you get through.
When they talk about recovery it's a thing
that people make out it's a decision
you just make and from then on forward
you don't make any mistakes.
But that's not what happens I'm afraid.
And that certainly doesn't
make the person any less brave.
For as long as your trying you are not failing
Do not let set backs discard
the progress you are making.
But what's also important to remember is
that it's okay if In recovery or journey
you don't have to have set backs
. What you went through/going through
is valid It's just awareness is what society lacks.
You think people loved you or cared about you.
Only because you were ill but even after
all this, people will love you still.
Your scared to take the jump because of the unknowns.
But you taking a leap of faith will be
the bravest act you have ever shown.

Day to day living with depression

Depression isn't just being sad it's a symptom of
a mental health condition that doctors and society
create an image that being depressed leaves
you bedridden, so if your not they don't listen.
Anorexia means you just don't want to eat.
Little do they know it's the hardest illness to beat.
Anxiety is rocking back and forth unable
to breathe on the floor but it is much more.
People can lose their life to this
And if they do people question and
say hang on what did I miss.
But they did say. You just dismissed
them telling them they'll be okay.
Sometimes there's nothing you can do,
no grand gestures or advice but t listen
because their minds can be like living in a prison.
With getting through each day feeling like a mission.
They don't want you to fix them
. They just don't want to battle alone again and again.
Depression looks like a smile or a laugh
A laugh that doesn't last.
A show so no one else knows.
There used to dealing with all this on there own.
So grab there's hand when they're in the dark
they'll pull away at first but as time goes on they
will soon find that there will be someone there.
No matter what goes on in there mind.
It will be a bit of a shock but eventually
they will let the guard down and the emotional block.
They'll learn not everyone's the same there will
be someone there when they are in pain.
They will realise they don't have to do this on there own
and one day they will make there way back home.

Being ill isn't your identity

Sometimes we can be scared to recover from mental health,
Because during the process we lost ourselves.
We don't know who we were before.
You think your mental health will be with you forevermore.
You think you illness is your identity but it is not.
There's more to you, and no not just a little but a lot.
You weren't born to be ill,
it was because things kind of went down hill.
Like a toddler with its dummy same applies
with your mental illness which may sound a bit
funny.
But it's true, like with the
dummy the toddler gets safety from.
Mental illness is where you get safety
from like a safety blanket,
so letting go of that will feel wrong. But you'll learn to belong without it.
Truth is after everything you've been through
you won't be the same.
But that's just what pain does it changes you
Shapes you into who you are.
One day you'll look back and see you've come so far.
In fact illness took
away the real you, your humour, personality.
You had to escape reality.
But don't be scared, because
now you can live a life if you just dared.
There will be people there that still care.
You maybe known as the Ill one.
But they don't love you or
care about you because of that part of you.
They love and care about you, because of all that you do
. Your smile, your humour, your kindness.
After this you may be different.
But is that bad, one day you'll wake up and be glad.
You Ignored that negative part of your
head a fought for a different life instead.
It was scary and at times really hard.
But you pushed through…and if you haven't just yet then…
I believe in you!

'River knows this there is no rush'

Winnie the Pooh has helped so many
people get through.
He said 'your smile is a reason for others to smile.'
Even if your smile hasn't been real for a while.
Pooh said. '
You must want to fly so much that
you are willing to give up being a caterpillar'
this always means giving up what's familiar.
'Perhaps the best thing to do is to stop writing Introductions
and get on with the book,
look sometimes it may seem easier
to stay in your corner of the forest.
But sometimes not all people
or thing comes to us so we have to go to them.
It can be scary but count to 10
Remember you're braver than you believe
stronger than you seem and smarter than
you think, sometimes the smallest things
take up the most room in your heart.
There will always be someone
to hold your hand in the dark.
We didn't realise we were making memories
, we just knew we were having fun.
These times can remind us that difficult times we can overcome.
Rivers know this there is no rush…

Loving little you

Close your eyes and imagine
your on a beach and your younger self you meet.
They come up to you and hug you and they have a massive smile,
a smile you've struggled to put on your own face for awhile.
They look at you and they tell you they love you.
And you tell them you love them too.
A little child is precious and beautiful
they're ever so small.
But had one of the biggest hearts.
They see your battle wounds
and says it looks like art.
You tell them your sorry and things
have been difficult to get through.
And they say '
I am beautiful just like you'
And that's when it clicked
like someone flicked a switch.
That's child is just the person you used to be
. Who used to want to be free who once believed
that anything she once dreamed
could be achieved.
You look at your younger self
they have that smile and that laugh,
they've always had that not matter
what went on in the past.
Something you'll learn in time is that with
self love and self acceptance combined
you will be able to learn to be kind to that
little girl or boy you'll be able to say
you didn't do anything wrong in fact
they couldn't be anymore strong.
They ask you to go make sandcastles in the sand that kid
is the only person that ever is going to understand

Guilt and shame

Guilt and shame is like my middle name.
I feel it all the time.
Normal things that I know every
human does.
Is like when I'm doing it,
I'm committing a crime.
I need to remind myself that
when thoughts like this come out of the blue
With no evidence
, to back up the thought up with.
Probably means it isn't even true.
To go against what your head
says is a scary thing
but why let you head win.
As people may or may
not have yet discovered.
But none of us have very
long in this world
Life isn't that as straight
forward to
what we were once told.
We all need to say a massive
f you to the world every now and then.
Life's hands us unnecessary
shit and expects us to deal with it.
Life's to short to cry over a bowl of pasta.
Or staying indoors because
'what's the point in going out for?'
Life's to short to listen to our head.
Or all the negative things
people may have once said.
Not everyone is going to like us and that's just the truth.
We just have to be grateful that over our heads
there's a roof. Some people don't even have that.
Life at times can be a loud of crap.
So never feel guilt or shame.
Eat the bowl of pasta. Or tell the person you love them.
Do the opposite
what your heads says
And live a life of freedom instead.
Do what you want, because
the only people you will disappoint is you.
So just do whatever the hell you want to do.

The happy one

Being the happy one, is hard when your finding
it hard to get through. And no matter how much
pain I'm in I wake up and i put on a smile i always do.
It takes a lot of strength to do that you know I
feel alone and not sure wether to come or go.
I'm in a confused state, with a lot on my plate.
I look like I have it all together but
lately I'm feeling under the weather.
With everything feeling grey.
With every how are you I answer always with
'I'm okay' Sometimes I wished someone could
see and say your not as happy as you seem to be
, seeing the real me.
Maybe someone will finally understand.
As they reach out there hand but there's a change I will push the hand
away because me well i'm always okay.
You know deep down this isn't true
but I'm in so much pain and no one has a clue.
People say they believe in me because
of all the things i've already got through
but there wrong if they believe that's why I'm 'strong.'
Mental health doesn't turn
you into a superhero, but a survivor.
A survivor of a mental health illness,
it doesn't make you fearless,
in fact it makes you fear the most.
Pushing away those that are close.
Your past trauma has made you a performer
. It's a defence mechanism.
The wall you've built around you is a mission to break down.
But one day you can't pretend your okay
so you fall to the ground.
And eventually you are found. So they wrap there arm around.
Wipe your eyes don't let them see
the person next to you isn't the person
you wished there to be. But they help you to breathe.
Your walls back up and you make some sarcastic joke or remark
They look you in the eyes while
you'll about to do that laugh and they don't be doing that lark.
And as you have that smile they ask if your okay and this is what you say...no.. no I'm not
okay but I didn't know how to say so a smile I portray. They hug you and you don't know
what to do. Not really remembering being hugged much before.
They help you off the floor.
It's hard to being the happy one
when your facing many battles your not sure you can overcome
. One day my laughter will turn to silence.
And that's when people will notice.
That's when I'll fall to the ground. As they'll realise I was the clown that was once in
town.And Now I've been found...

Feel the fear do it anyway

You feel like you deserve bad things.
Sometimes it feels easier to let your head win.
When you don't listen your head and the thoughts get louder
And when you listen to your head it gets prouder.
But the thoughts get unbearable and strong.
But that's only because your heads scared
you will find out that your head is wrong
. That you do actually belong.
Scared you'll figure out all it's little lies,
scared you'll no longer be on its side.
People may have hurt you so you think you
deserve that but you don't you think people will
abandon you but they won't
. It may have been bad in the past but that doesn't
mean you don't deserve a chance
to live life and laugh and for it to last.
Mental health is a difficult monster to face
but one day you will realise you were
never meant to go through all this in the first place.
You will fight for another life instead.
Instead of always listening to your head.
Because it's wrong. And your strong
and to get through all this you have to brave
but it also is okay to be afraid doesn't mean you can't do it take it but by bit.
Your not alone don't go through this on your own.
Stare the monster in the eyes and fight even if you can't see the light.
Feel the fear and do it anyway.
Maybe just maybe things will actually be okay.

Don't lose that kids spark

Do you remember when we put our arms in our shirts
and pretend we had no arms.
Or would play our favourite song as our alarm.
Pouring soda into a cap and pretend like it's shots
And cuddling all your teddy bears
at night because you didn't want
to leave any out even when you had lots.
Remember when you had those pens
that had multiple colours and you'd try push them down at the same time.
Remember in a hall in school
singing shine Jesus shine.
Remember when it was raining and rain
drops in the window would have a race.
Remember when you'd argue with siblings
because you sat in a specific seat on the sofa
and they knick your place or who would
press the button on the lift or when they'd steal
your clothes now that was taking the piss.
Going shopping and running and swinging on the Tesco trolly
Going on school trips and having those milk lolly's.
Going to blockbusters picking a film for movie night.
Or at Christmas seeing all the lights
Why do we have to grow up?
That's what I want to know?
Where did all those times go?
We may need to grow but that doesn't
mean we have to act all serious and lose that kids
spark it's madness and silliness that gets us out of the dark.
So don't lose that.

Attention seeking

When babies cry they're seeking
attention from their loved ones.
Or their mums.
When someone struggles with mental Health illness
they are called attention-seeking, which has a
different meaning to a baby seeking attention.
But attention doesn't have to be a bad/
negative thing can I just mention.
We all need attention to survive.
It's like tinker bell
without attention she would die.
Some people with mental health
can regress to a young age.
Because maybe the love and affection
they need they didn't get to that stage.
Now I'm saying that we all should attention
seek but saying your struggling or
asking for help doesn't make you weak.
If your struggling/ have struggled with this
phrase then I'm letting you know that it's
okay let them say whatever they want to say.
Remember if your crying as a baby you
were just needing your basic human
needs met maybe.
Well not maybe you were.
Attention seeking is just a biological imperative
Yet it is a negative selfish thing is
the narrative when I fact it's like it was when we were a baby
It's about our needs, nothing about greed

Don't let damage control you

When we have struggled with mental
health for so long healing or recovery can feel wrong
Healing can make us feel like a liar
or it invalidates everything that's we've been through.
But everything we needed to
do to recover no one had a clue.
I saw a quote that read, healing doesn't
mean the damage never existed
, it just means the damage no longer controls you.
And that couldn't be any more true.
All the pain and upset you didn't deserve
And yes maybe at some point the unhealthy
coping mechanisms
had a purpose it did serve.
But we get to a point we don't need
them anymore, we start to question why are we doing this for,
And sometimes
we need to let go and know life's full of unknowns
Change can be scary,
it's easy for things to stay the same. We adapt to the pain.
But that is not living or being free
but it's easier to stay because a life of happiness
or freedom we don't believe can be achieved,
but for as long as you are breathing there is
hope no matter how hard you're finding it to cope.
When you are scared that's exactly when you take
the leap of faith it may feel uncomfortable
or may not feel right
but your on your way to finding the light in life.
Remember healing doesn't mean the damage
never existed it means
the damage no longer controls you.
Take the leap of faith, feel the fear do
it anyone because you have a lot of thing that you have left to do...
I believe in you

One percent

A nurse said to me you can't see
past this can you? I was like no.
She shared her own struggle with mental health.
She was like 99% of her was caught up on
it never getting better. But she had 1%
that believed she can. And as long
as she had that one percent she was okay
. And that 1% was the reason why
she kept going.
And she would give that to other people.
On days she needed that 1%
she was like you don't need to tell
people you need that 1% just get someone
. She was like even if you don't want to get better
you have it in you too.
Even if it's not what you want
you just have to grab onto the 1% and keep fighting
even if it's the last thing you want to do.
1 % may not be a lot compared to
the 99% that wants to give up or see no hope but as
long as you have 1% hold onto that.

What heals the heart

We think it's happiness that is important and
yes it is to a certain degree but is
happiness what we need to heal a heart I
wouldn't completely agree.
If we go and visit someone who's
unwell we are not doing that because it
would bring us happiness we do
it because it matters to us…they matter to us
Doing this that matter to us is a must
Maybe to heal a
heart is doing a piece of art
Or maybe listening to your favourite
song when nights are so long.
Maybe having someone there
when you can no longer be strong
even if it feels wrong then letting you
know you belong, someone being there
Someone saying they care
even if that itself gives you a bit of a scare.
Someone
loving you the right way
Making sure you are okay but
also loving yourself and if you're doing something
That heals your heart then forget about everything else
The question to what heals the heart
is different for everyone, everyone is facing
battles there trying to overcome,
Everyone's hearts there trying to fix there own.
I guess that's why it's always remember to know your not alone.
It's not about being
the happiest person,
We set so many high standards for ourselves
that are impossible to reach, doing the
things that matter to us we should preach.
Being with someone you love the most
Sitting with your partner or by yourself watching
the sunset by the coast
So what heals a heart
Maybe the answers are within our selfs
No where else…

Validation

The alcoholic who stops drinking is still struggling
The anorexic who is a healthy weight or
who has been a
healthy weight throughout is still struggling
The depressed person who got out of bed
and washed is still struggling
Behaviours may have stopped it's
not to say the thoughts have stopped.
In fact they are still raging and roaring
And some days tears still pouring.
We don't need invalidation we need appreciation.
We are trying to beat the deadliest of beats even
when we have accepted defat.
But we keep going and going with a smile still
showing still facing the battle
without anyone knowing
But if your reading this and fighting the battle
but disengaged in behaviours I know your still struggling I know.
And your not alone.
Society create and image and on how someone with
mental health is meant to be and we look at
that image or narrative and think well that isn't me.
Don't discard your mental
health and look after yourself.
Mental health is more then
meets the eye it isn't made up or a lie
It's not just a fun term I hope that people stopping
behaviours doesn't mean there thoughts have
necessary stopped and I hope this is something people learn.
You kept going and fighting even when the battle you
didn't think you could overcome even when
your head could of won. That's brave
you kept going despite being so afraid
I'm proud of you and I Thank-you so much for pushing through
Anything you've been through is valid enough because you have suffered.

Acceptance

Loving ourselves
isn't what we need
to do maybe that's where
we have got it wrong,
We need to accept
that we belong
No matter if you have
ache or spots or lines on your face
No matter
what your race
Some things aren't meant to be
changed about us in the first place
Accept and grow
Acceptance is key
one day I hope you see
We are our own worst
enemy so just breathe
And if people can't accept you
then well they can leave
Happiness suits you, you know
So let yourself grow
You're fine just the way you are.
Shine just like a star.

One more day

What If you were to stay just one more day
Even though it's grey
Even if staying won't make the
pain go straight away
But what if you just stay
one more day.
I know you're tired you don't
want to do it anymore
But what if you get up and try just one more time
Even if keeping ongoing feels like a crime.
What If you just didn't give up and you
say enough is enough
I'm going to do it for those that I love but also for you
What a flipping brave
thing that is t do.
Giving up seems like
the only way out
And keeping on going is difficult there is no doubt
But what if you just kept going anyway
And what if things actually
do become okay
What if you do eventually get out the grey
To get out of bed instead of listening to your head.
To do this battle and over come and by the
end you can say 'I have won'
To engage in a battle of war and even if
you ask yourself what for
You may have accepted defeat but this you can
beat ask yourself will the fight be one day? or will it be day one?
And fight to overcome
Please choose today and I hope you choose to stay.

Unopened Post

When going through mental health, eating disorders,
Depression, being an alcoholic.
We use the alcohol or self-harm
To make us feel calm.
It numbs the pain.
How? Well, it's difficult to explain.
Think of struggles or trauma like receiving
letters through the letterbox.
Over time letters pile up on the floor.
Do we want to sit and open them we are unsure?
There comes
more and more and more.
You see mental health drugs
alcohol self-harm deflects us from that.
Distracts us or numbs us from
all the post that's on the welcome mat.
But as we let go of those mechanisms
we start to look through the post on the ground
Opening all the letters
Now, this isn't easy.
All the letters aren't an easy read.
But they're important to go through indeed.
We can stop reading
them let them to continue to gather up in a pile
Or we can go the extra mile.
And to try and stay strong even when it feels wrong
To keep reading, I know inside
you maybe bleeding. Hurting to
the core wondering why your doing this for.
But to open the front door to the world you
need to get through the letters and post on the floor.
We all have unopened post.
We need to go through those that matter most.
Letting go of self harm alcohol drugs
We are opening the letters.
And you can wipe your salty tears with your sweaters.
It's not an easy thing to do and you may not have a clue
But open one letter at a time and you will soon find
You have to learn to be kind to yourself
Don't worry about anyone else
Open your post
Open the door and go and explore

Battle field

I kept facing the world head on,
Even though at times it felt wrong
I battled through even when I didn't want to
even when keeping on going I didn't have a clue how to do
But here I am.
Nights got longer but I grew stronger.
Some days I wanted to disappear,
Thoughts so loud but my friends say
'I am here' catching every tear.
When I have them I don't have to be in fear
Mental health is a constant battle of war
We think we will have to fight forevermore.
Think of it as if your on a battle field and
your unhealthy coping mechanisms are your shield.
You see when you don't engage in the thoughts or behaviour
You gain a troop and the other team which is your mental illness,
Is now a man down.
And you're on your journey to being found
And every time you ignore the
thought there's another troop added
to your team and it'll be the strongest team ever to be seen.
In a war someone has to win but that's the thing.
What about a draw?
And putting the weapons down on the floor
and walking away and this is what you say
'It's hard to fight and right now I can't see the light.'
But you put down your weapons not to accept defeat
but to accept this maybe how it is right now
Disengaged in a battle of war because the other side is asking
for more and more.
But the more you don't listen or to not act or
the thoughts in your brain the more
troops to have to deal with the pain your other alone in this
you know don't go through it on your own.
In this war there will always be a medic by your side.
Remember this when ever your in a battle and cried.
Please survive.

Look at you

Look at you,
look at how the world has treated you,
But what do you do?
You help others get through,
No matter how bad you have been treated,
you are still not defeated,
You spread love and care all around
even when you yourself have fallen to the ground,
Do you know how rare that is.
I mean the world has given you every reason to hate it,
to be angry and upset,
But kindness and compassion everyone gets.
You don't concentrate on the bad things and let your head win
You show the world that bad things
can and will happen in life but you will get back up,
And you are enough,
Life is tough,
No matter what life has thrown
or times you've felt alone,
You still have a heart of gold
even though life's not like what you were told.
Maybe the love and care you afford to give to others
you can give that to yourself,
Because you deserve that just like everyone else
the world needs you,
Needs your truth,
When people have self doubt/ no hope.
They can look at you and see your living proof,
No matter the storm or the rain
pouring down on the ground,
There's always a change to turn it all around.

Looking monsters in the face

A friend said to me the other day
' you look monsters dead in the face,
just so others can make it home safe.'
No matter what's I'm going through.
Being there for people I always try to do.
Now I'm not saying this to try and portray
myself as a good person or out of spite.
But I know how sometimes it can be hard to see the light.
Sometimes we face monsters because
Of someone you love or someone else
And we forget to face the monsters
because of ourselves.
I don't know why I face my monsters
Every single day.
Because I don't even think things will be okay.
But to other people that's all I ever say.
Epically if I contributed I love seeing people
make it home safe.
It helps me to not just think I'm just this waste of space.
This maybe something have to do on my own
. But one day, maybe one day
I will too make my way back home.

It wasn't your fault

You know it weren't your fault right?
It wasn't your fault what happened
And the thought that you think that makes me saddened.
The thought that you think no one can love you because of the past
Or maybe you feel like the love won't last.
Truth is you were let down.
And now your surrounded by thoughts
and feelings that feel like your going to drown.
But you can turn it around.
But you need to learn you are not to blame
that the people that hurt you should be ashamed.
Of themselves and not you.
You were a kid/ teenager and they didn't do the job
they were meant to do.
And now it maybe hard to let people in but don't let
those people who hurt you win.
Look how far you have come
All that hurt and pain and wanting to run.
But here you are you've come this far.
Be who you want to be. And one day you will feel free.
You will learn the truth, that it was them and not you.
And that will be your breakthrough.

Channel that energy

Anger
, now anger can be seen as something that is terrible.
The women who fought for women's rights
anger was unmeasurable.
And it was what they did with it that matters
They held onto anger and frustration and embodied change.
They fought for something which at the time felt strange.
They did what they thought was best
And ignored The rest.
Now something/ someone can make us angry
but we shouldn't let that impact or destroy us but to use that energy
Into poetry, or a speech, or to change the world or a piece of art
Let that anger pour out of your heart
Instead of letting that anger take over
or destroy ourselves focus that energy into something else

Breaking down the wall

When going through pain we can build up
the walls we build it higher and higher
when something hurts us even when It's small.
We've built up this wall for months maybe even
years pushing away anyone that comes near
It's easier that way then being hurt or in fear
Too scared to make connections because the fear of rejection.
It took a long time to build up that wall it's a
protective factor so t won't be easy to break down at all.
But if you take one brick down at a time
you'll learn or you'll discover it's fine.
If you've been hurt before then it makes us feel like we have
to do things on our own.
Although the comfort the wall brings it can make us feel alone
. How to break it down when we were never shown.
Rome wasn't built in a day and neither was the wall
built in the day but that doesn't mean
you can't break it down and be okay.
It's okay to be scared anxious or hurt but let people
love you and care Even if it gives you a bit of a scare.
They say it's better to have loved and lost then to never have loved at all
So maybe it's about time to start breaking down that wall

Stigma

Mental health has a massive stigma around.
We ignore them and tell them it's normal to feel down.
With OCD, people say we all have a little bit
of OCD in us which I wouldn't completely
agree maybe to a certain degree
But it's not OCD we all have perfectionism which is a symptom
of OCD, OCD can be a coping mechanism you see
Those with depression are bed ridden but in reality
Someone with depressions pain stays hidden
Those with an eating disorder aren't always
underweight which may make people debate.
But people die from this disorder when do we help them when it's too late.
Some people can suffers with suicidal
Thoughts yet not act on those
As they don't want to hurt those that are close.
Those with anxiety just worry too much
What people don't realise mental health can become like an invisible crutch.
your letting go of a part of you that taught you
how to survive, with the perception
is you suffer with mental health or depression you won't be able to thrive.
Or amount to much in life.
Which isn't at all true
. There's many people out there trying
to get through who have struggled/ are struggling and we never even knew.
People who suffers get called weak but how
are they weak fighting a battle everyday they are trying to beat when they could of
easily accepted defeat.
If you look at MRI scans of those who are
enduring mental health you can see the damage the impact In the brain.
So think about that next time you stereotype
or invalidate someone's pain.
You've suffered so your valid enough.
Look at you keeping on going even when things are so tough.

'Quite frankly zoe the world needs you in it
You have a voice a powerful
voice and everyone needs to hear it.'
That was said to me a few months ago
and here's me sharing my voice to the world...
Love zoe x

;

Printed in Great Britain
by Amazon

79685215R00048